VISIT OUR WEBSITE

Learn more about our mission and find our latest updates, hot new releases, freebies, and more.

www.thebubble.press

DON'T FORGET TO RATE THE PRODUCT

AND LEAVE A REVIEW.

We care about your opinion!

Help us improve our products.

The Bubble Press

All of our products are crafted
with obsessive attention to detail.

Book Titles

01 ....

02 ....

03 ....

04 ....

05 ....

06 ....

07 ....

08 ....

09 ....

10 ....

11 ....

12 ....

13 ....

14 ....

15 ....

16 ....

17 ....

18 ....

19 ....

20 ....

Book Titles

21 ....

22 ....

23 ....

24 ....

25 ....

26 ....

27 ....

28 ....

29 ....

30 ....

31 ....

32 ....

33 ....

34 ....

35 ....

36 ....

37 ....

38 ....

39 ....

40 ....

Book Titles

41 ....

42 ....

43 ....

44 ....

45 ....

46 ....

47 ....

48 ....

49 ....

50 ....

51 ....

52 ....

53 ....

54 ....

55 ....

56 ....

57 ....

58 ....

59 ....

60 ....

Book Titles

61 ....

62 ....

63 ....

64 ....

65 ....

66 ....

67 ....

68 ....

69 ....

70 ....

71 ....

72 ....

73 ....

74 ....

75 ....

76 ....

77 ....

78 ....

79 ....

80 ....

Book Titles

81 ....

82 ....

83 ....

84 ....

85 ....

86 ....

87 ....

88 ....

89 ....

90 ....

91 ....

92 ....

93 ....

94 ....

95 ....

96 ....

97 ....

98 ....

99 ....

100 ....

☐ Paperback ☐ Hardback ☐ Ebook ☐ Audiobook

☐ Non-fiction ☐ Fiction

1

Started: .... Finished: ....

Book Title: ....

Author: ....

My Review

....

....

....

....

....

My Favorite Character: ....

Best part of the book:

....

....

....

....

Favorite Quotes From the Book:

....

....

....

....

Source:

☐ Bought ☐ loaned

From ....

The book was easy to read

☐ Yes   ☐ No

Would you recommend
this book to a friend?

☐ Yes   ☐ No

Rating ☆ ☆ ☆ ☆ ☆

☐ Paperback ☐ Hardback ☐ Ebook ☐ Audiobook

☐ Non-fiction ☐ Fiction

2

Started: .... Finished: ....

Book Title: ....

Author: ....

My Review

....

....

....

....

....

My Favorite Character: ....

Best part of the book:

....

....

....

....

Favorite Quotes From the Book:

....

....

....

....

Source:

☐ Bought ☐ loaned

From ....

The book was easy to read

☐ Yes   ☐ No

Would you recommend
this book to a friend?

☐ Yes   ☐ No

Rating ☆ ☆ ☆ ☆ ☆

☐ Paperback ☐ Hardback ☐ Ebook ☐ Audiobook

☐ Non-fiction ☐ Fiction

3

Started: .... Finished: ....

Book Title: ....

Author: ....

My Review

....

....

....

....

....

My Favorite Character: ....

Best part of the book:

....

....

....

....

Favorite Quotes From the Book:

....

....

....

....

Source:

☐ Bought ☐ loaned

From ....

The book was easy to read

☐ Yes   ☐ No

Would you recommend this book to a friend?

☐ Yes   ☐ No

Rating   ☆ ☆ ☆ ☆ ☆

☐ Paperback ☐ Hardback ☐ Ebook ☐ Audiobook

☐ Non-fiction ☐ Fiction

4

Started: .... Finished: ....

Book Title: ....

Author: ....

My Review

....

....

....

....

....

My Favorite Character: ....

Best part of the book:

....

....

....

....

Favorite Quotes From the Book:

....

....

....

....

Source:

☐ Bought ☐ loaned

From ....

The book was easy to read

☐ Yes   ☐ No

Would you recommend
this book to a friend?

☐ Yes   ☐ No

Rating ☆ ☆ ☆ ☆ ☆

☐ Paperback ☐ Hardback ☐ Ebook ☐ Audiobook

☐ Non-fiction ☐ Fiction

5

Started: .... Finished: ....

Book Title: ....

Author: ....

My Review

....

....

....

....

....

My Favorite Character: ....

Best part of the book:

....

....

....

....

Favorite Quotes From the Book:

....

....

....

....

Source:

☐ Bought ☐ loaned

From ....

The book was easy to read

☐ Yes ☐ No

Would you recommend this book to a friend?

☐ Yes ☐ No

Rating ☆ ☆ ☆ ☆ ☆

☐ Paperback ☐ Hardback ☐ Ebook ☐ Audiobook

☐ Non-fiction ☐ Fiction

6

Started: .... Finished: ....

Book Title: ....

Author: ....

My Review

....

....

....

....

....

My Favorite Character: ....

Best part of the book:

....

....

....

....

Favorite Quotes From the Book:

....

....

....

....

Source:

☐ Bought ☐ loaned

From ....

The book was easy to read

☐ Yes   ☐ No

Would you recommend
this book to a friend?

☐ Yes   ☐ No

Rating ☆ ☆ ☆ ☆ ☆

☐ Paperback ☐ Hardback ☐ Ebook ☐ Audiobook

☐ Non-fiction ☐ Fiction

7

Started: .... Finished: ....

Book Title: ....

Author: ....

My Review

....

....

....

....

....

My Favorite Character: ....

Best part of the book:

....

....

....

....

Favorite Quotes From the Book:

....

....

....

....

Source:

☐ Bought ☐ loaned

From ....

The book was easy to read

☐ Yes   ☐ No

Would you recommend this book to a friend?

☐ Yes   ☐ No

Rating ☆ ☆ ☆ ☆ ☆

○ Paperback ○ Hardback ○ Ebook ○ Audiobook

○ Non-fiction ○ Fiction

8

Started: .... Finished: ....

Book Title: ....

Author: ....

My Review

....

....

....

....

....

My Favorite Character: ....

Best part of the book:

....

....

....

....

Favorite Quotes From the Book:

....

....

....

....

Source:

○ Bought ○ loaned

From ....

The book was easy to read

○ Yes   ○ No

Would you recommend this book to a friend?

○ Yes   ○ No

Rating ☆ ☆ ☆ ☆ ☆

☐ Paperback ☐ Hardback ☐ Ebook ☐ Audiobook

☐ Non-fiction ☐ Fiction

9

Started: .... Finished: ....

Book Title: ....

Author: ....

My Review

....
....
....
....
....

My Favorite Character: ....

Best part of the book:

....
....
....
....

Favorite Quotes From the Book:

....
....
....
....

Source:

☐ Bought ☐ loaned

From ....

The book was easy to read

☐ Yes   ☐ No

Would you recommend
this book to a friend?

☐ Yes   ☐ No

Rating   ☆ ☆ ☆ ☆ ☆

○ Paperback ○ Hardback ○ Ebook ○ Audiobook

○ Non-fiction ○ Fiction

10

Started: .... Finished: ....

Book Title: ....

Author: ....

My Review

....

....

....

....

....

My Favorite Character: ....

Best part of the book:

....

....

....

....

Favorite Quotes From the Book:

....

....

....

....

Source:

○ Bought ○ loaned

From ....

The book was easy to read

○ Yes   ○ No

Would you recommend
this book to a friend?

○ Yes   ○ No

Rating ☆ ☆ ☆ ☆ ☆

○ Paperback ○ Hardback ○ Ebook ○ Audiobook

○ Non-fiction ○ Fiction

11

Started: .... Finished: ....

Book Title: ....

Author: ....

My Review

....

....

....

....

....

My Favorite Character: ....

Best part of the book:

....

....

....

....

Favorite Quotes From the Book:

....

....

....

....

Source:

○ Bought ○ loaned

From ....

The book was easy to read

○ Yes   ○ No

Would you recommend
this book to a friend?

○ Yes   ○ No

Rating ☆ ☆ ☆ ☆ ☆

○ Paperback ○ Hardback ○ Ebook ○ Audiobook

○ Non-fiction ○ Fiction

12

Started: .... Finished: ....

Book Title: ....

Author: ....

My Review

....

....

....

....

....

My Favorite Character: ....

Best part of the book:

....

....

....

....

Favorite Quotes From the Book:

....

....

....

....

Source:

○ Bought ○ loaned

From ....

The book was easy to read

○ Yes   ○ No

Would you recommend
this book to a friend?

○ Yes   ○ No

Rating   ☆ ☆ ☆ ☆ ☆

○ Paperback ○ Hardback ○ Ebook ○ Audiobook

○ Non-fiction ○ Fiction

13

Started: .... Finished: ....

Book Title: ....

Author: ....

My Review

....
....
....
....
....

My Favorite Character: ....

Best part of the book:

....
....
....
....

Favorite Quotes From the Book:

....
....
....
....

Source:

○ Bought ○ loaned

From ....

The book was easy to read

○ Yes ○ No

Would you recommend this book to a friend?

○ Yes ○ No

Rating ☆ ☆ ☆ ☆ ☆

☐ Paperback ☐ Hardback ☐ Ebook ☐ Audiobook

☐ Non-fiction ☐ Fiction

14

Started: .... Finished: ....

Book Title: ....

Author: ....

My Review

....
....
....
....
....

My Favorite Character: ....

Best part of the book:

....
....
....
....

Favorite Quotes From the Book:

....
....
....
....

Source:

☐ Bought ☐ loaned

From ....

The book was easy to read

☐ Yes   ☐ No

Would you recommend
this book to a friend?

☐ Yes   ☐ No

Rating ☆ ☆ ☆ ☆ ☆

☐ Paperback ☐ Hardback ☐ Ebook ☐ Audiobook

☐ Non-fiction ☐ Fiction

15

Started: .... Finished: ....

Book Title: ....

Author: ....

My Review

....
....
....
....
....

My Favorite Character: ....

Best part of the book:

....
....
....
....

Favorite Quotes From the Book:

....
....
....
....

Source:

☐ Bought ☐ loaned

From ....

The book was easy to read

☐ Yes   ☐ No

Would you recommend
this book to a friend?

☐ Yes   ☐ No

Rating ☆ ☆ ☆ ☆ ☆

☐ Paperback ☐ Hardback ☐ Ebook ☐ Audiobook

☐ Non-fiction ☐ Fiction

16

Started: .... Finished: ....

Book Title: ....

Author: ....

My Review

....

....

....

....

....

My Favorite Character: ....

Best part of the book:

....

....

....

....

Favorite Quotes From the Book:

....

....

....

....

Source:

☐ Bought ☐ loaned

From ....

The book was easy to read

☐ Yes ☐ No

Would you recommend this book to a friend?

☐ Yes ☐ No

Rating ☆ ☆ ☆ ☆ ☆

☐ Paperback ☐ Hardback ☐ Ebook ☐ Audiobook

☐ Non-fiction ☐ Fiction

17

Started: .... Finished: ....

Book Title: ....

Author: ....

My Review

....

....

....

....

....

My Favorite Character: ....

Best part of the book:

....

....

....

....

Favorite Quotes From the Book:

....

....

....

....

Source:

☐ Bought ☐ loaned

From ....

The book was easy to read

☐ Yes   ☐ No

Would you recommend
this book to a friend?

☐ Yes   ☐ No

Rating ☆ ☆ ☆ ☆ ☆

☐ Paperback ☐ Hardback ☐ Ebook ☐ Audiobook

☐ Non-fiction ☐ Fiction

18

Started: .... Finished: ....

Book Title: ....

Author: ....

My Review

....
....
....
....
....

My Favorite Character: ....

Best part of the book:

....

....

....

....

Favorite Quotes From the Book:

....

....

....

....

Source:

☐ Bought ☐ loaned

From ....

The book was easy to read

☐ Yes   ☐ No

Would you recommend this book to a friend?

☐ Yes   ☐ No

Rating ☆ ☆ ☆ ☆ ☆

☐ Paperback ☐ Hardback ☐ Ebook ☐ Audiobook

☐ Non-fiction ☐ Fiction

19

Started: .... Finished: ....

Book Title: ....

Author: ....

My Review

....

....

....

....

....

My Favorite Character: ....

Best part of the book:

....

....

....

....

Favorite Quotes From the Book:

....

....

....

....

Source:

☐ Bought ☐ loaned

From ....

The book was easy to read

☐ Yes ☐ No

Would you recommend this book to a friend?

☐ Yes ☐ No

Rating ☆ ☆ ☆ ☆ ☆

☐ Paperback ☐ Hardback ☐ Ebook ☐ Audiobook

☐ Non-fiction ☐ Fiction

20

Started: .... Finished: ....

Book Title: ....

Author: ....

My Review

....
....
....
....
....

My Favorite Character: ....

Best part of the book:

....
....
....
....

Favorite Quotes From the Book:

....
....
....
....

Source:

☐ Bought ☐ loaned

From ....

The book was easy to read

☐ Yes ☐ No

Would you recommend this book to a friend?

☐ Yes ☐ No

Rating ☆ ☆ ☆ ☆ ☆

☐ Paperback   ☐ Hardback   ☐ Ebook   ☐ Audiobook

☐ Non-fiction   ☐ Fiction

21

Started: .... Finished: ....

Book Title: ....

Author: ....

My Review

....

....

....

....

....

My Favorite Character: ....

Best part of the book:

....

....

....

....

Favorite Quotes From the Book:

....

....

....

....

Source:

☐ Bought   ☐ loaned

From ....

The book was easy to read

☐ Yes   ☐ No

Would you recommend
this book to a friend?

☐ Yes   ☐ No

Rating   ☆☆☆☆☆

☐ Paperback ☐ Hardback ☐ Ebook ☐ Audiobook

☐ Non-fiction ☐ Fiction

22

Started: .... Finished: ....

Book Title: ....

Author: ....

My Review

....

....

....

....

....

My Favorite Character: ....

Best part of the book:

....

....

....

....

Favorite Quotes From the Book:

....

....

....

....

Source:

☐ Bought ☐ loaned

From ....

The book was easy to read

☐ Yes ☐ No

Would you recommend this book to a friend?

☐ Yes ☐ No

Rating ☆ ☆ ☆ ☆ ☆

☐ Paperback ☐ Hardback ☐ Ebook ☐ Audiobook

☐ Non-fiction ☐ Fiction

23

Started: .... Finished: ....

Book Title: ....

Author: ....

My Review

....
....
....
....
....

My Favorite Character: ....

Best part of the book:

....
....
....
....

Favorite Quotes From the Book:

....
....
....
....

Source:

☐ Bought ☐ loaned

From ....

The book was easy to read

☐ Yes   ☐ No

Would you recommend
this book to a friend?

☐ Yes   ☐ No

Rating ☆ ☆ ☆ ☆ ☆

☐ Paperback ☐ Hardback ☐ Ebook ☐ Audiobook

☐ Non-fiction ☐ Fiction

24

Started: .... Finished: ....

Book Title: ....

Author: ....

My Review

....

....

....

....

....

My Favorite Character: ....

Best part of the book:

....

....

....

....

Favorite Quotes From the Book:

....

....

....

....

Source:

☐ Bought ☐ loaned

From ....

The book was easy to read

☐ Yes   ☐ No

Would you recommend this book to a friend?

☐ Yes   ☐ No

Rating ☆ ☆ ☆ ☆ ☆

☐ Paperback ☐ Hardback ☐ Ebook ☐ Audiobook

☐ Non-fiction ☐ Fiction

25

Started: .... Finished: ....

Book Title: ....

Author: ....

My Review

....
....
....
....
....

My Favorite Character: ....

Best part of the book:

....
....
....
....

Favorite Quotes From the Book:

....
....
....
....

Source:

☐ Bought ☐ loaned

From ....

The book was easy to read

☐ Yes   ☐ No

Would you recommend this book to a friend?

☐ Yes   ☐ No

Rating ☆☆☆☆☆

○ Paperback ○ Hardback ○ Ebook ○ Audiobook

○ Non-fiction ○ Fiction

26

Started: .... Finished: ....

Book Title: ....

Author: ....

My Review

....

....

....

....

....

My Favorite Character: ....

Best part of the book:

....

....

....

....

Favorite Quotes From the Book:

....

....

....

....

Source:

○ Bought ○ loaned

From ....

The book was easy to read

○ Yes ○ No

Would you recommend this book to a friend?

○ Yes ○ No

Rating ☆ ☆ ☆ ☆ ☆

☐ Paperback ☐ Hardback ☐ Ebook ☐ Audiobook

☐ Non-fiction ☐ Fiction

27

Started: .... Finished: ....

Book Title: ....

Author: ....

My Review

....

....

....

....

....

My Favorite Character: ....

Best part of the book:

....

....

....

....

Favorite Quotes From the Book:

....

....

....

....

Source:

☐ Bought ☐ loaned

From ....

The book was easy to read

☐ Yes   ☐ No

Would you recommend
this book to a friend?

☐ Yes   ☐ No

Rating ☆ ☆ ☆ ☆ ☆

☐ Paperback ☐ Hardback ☐ Ebook ☐ Audiobook

☐ Non-fiction ☐ Fiction

28

Started: .... Finished: ....

Book Title: ....

Author: ....

My Review

....

....

....

....

....

My Favorite Character: ....

Best part of the book:

....

....

....

....

Favorite Quotes From the Book:

....

....

....

....

Source:

☐ Bought ☐ loaned

From ....

The book was easy to read

☐ Yes   ☐ No

Would you recommend
this book to a friend?

☐ Yes   ☐ No

Rating   ☆ ☆ ☆ ☆ ☆

○ Paperback ○ Hardback ○ Ebook ○ Audiobook

○ Non-fiction ○ Fiction

29

Started: .... Finished: ....

Book Title: ....

Author: ....

My Review

....

....

....

....

....

My Favorite Character: ....

Best part of the book:

....

....

....

....

Favorite Quotes From the Book:

....

....

....

....

Source:

○ Bought ○ loaned

From ....

The book was easy to read

○ Yes ○ No

Would you recommend this book to a friend?

○ Yes ○ No

Rating ☆ ☆ ☆ ☆ ☆

☐ Paperback ☐ Hardback ☐ Ebook ☐ Audiobook

☐ Non-fiction ☐ Fiction

30

Started: .... Finished: ....

Book Title: ....

Author: ....

My Review

....

....

....

....

....

My Favorite Character: ....

Best part of the book:

....

....

....

....

Favorite Quotes From the Book:

....

....

....

....

Source:

☐ Bought ☐ loaned

From ....

The book was easy to read

☐ Yes ☐ No

Would you recommend this book to a friend?

☐ Yes ☐ No

Rating ☆ ☆ ☆ ☆ ☆

☐ Paperback ☐ Hardback ☐ Ebook ☐ Audiobook

☐ Non-fiction ☐ Fiction

31

Started: .... Finished: ....

Book Title: ....

Author: ....

My Review

....

....

....

....

....

My Favorite Character: ....

Best part of the book:

....

....

....

....

Favorite Quotes From the Book:

....

....

....

....

Source:

☐ Bought ☐ loaned

From ....

The book was easy to read

☐ Yes   ☐ No

Would you recommend this book to a friend?

☐ Yes   ☐ No

Rating ☆ ☆ ☆ ☆ ☆

○ Paperback ○ Hardback ○ Ebook ○ Audiobook

○ Non-fiction ○ Fiction

32

Started: .... Finished: ....

Book Title: ....

Author: ....

My Review

....

....

....

....

....

My Favorite Character: ....

Best part of the book:

....

....

....

....

Favorite Quotes From the Book:

....

....

....

....

Source:

○ Bought ○ loaned

From ....

The book was easy to read

○ Yes   ○ No

Would you recommend this book to a friend?

○ Yes   ○ No

Rating ☆ ☆ ☆ ☆ ☆

☐ Paperback ☐ Hardback ☐ Ebook ☐ Audiobook

☐ Non-fiction ☐ Fiction

33

Started: .... Finished: ....

Book Title: ....

Author: ....

My Review

....

....

....

....

....

My Favorite Character: ....

Best part of the book:

....

....

....

....

Favorite Quotes From the Book:

....

....

....

....

Source:

☐ Bought ☐ loaned

From ....

The book was easy to read

☐ Yes   ☐ No

Would you recommend
this book to a friend?

☐ Yes   ☐ No

Rating ☆ ☆ ☆ ☆ ☆

○ Paperback ○ Hardback ○ Ebook ○ Audiobook

○ Non-fiction ○ Fiction

34

Started: .... Finished: ....

Book Title: ....

Author: ....

My Review

....

....

....

....

....

My Favorite Character: ....

Best part of the book:

....

....

....

....

Favorite Quotes From the Book:

....

....

....

....

Source:

○ Bought ○ loaned

From ....

The book was easy to read

○ Yes ○ No

Would you recommend this book to a friend?

○ Yes ○ No

Rating ☆ ☆ ☆ ☆ ☆

○ Paperback ○ Hardback ○ Ebook ○ Audiobook

○ Non-fiction ○ Fiction

35

Started: .... Finished: ....

Book Title: ....

Author: ....

My Review

....

....

....

....

....

My Favorite Character: ....

Best part of the book:

....

....

....

....

Favorite Quotes From the Book:

....

....

....

....

Source:

○ Bought ○ loaned

From ....

The book was easy to read

○ Yes   ○ No

Would you recommend
this book to a friend?

○ Yes   ○ No

Rating ☆ ☆ ☆ ☆ ☆

☐ Paperback ☐ Hardback ☐ Ebook ☐ Audiobook

☐ Non-fiction ☐ Fiction

36

Started: .... Finished: ....

Book Title: ....

Author: ....

My Review

....

....

....

....

....

My Favorite Character: ....

Best part of the book:

....

....

....

....

Favorite Quotes From the Book:

....

....

....

....

Source:

☐ Bought ☐ loaned

From ....

The book was easy to read

☐ Yes ☐ No

Would you recommend
this book to a friend?

☐ Yes ☐ No

Rating ☆☆☆☆☆

○ Paperback ○ Hardback ○ Ebook ○ Audiobook

○ Non-fiction ○ Fiction

37

Started: .... Finished: ....

Book Title: ....

Author: ....

My Review

....

....

....

....

....

My Favorite Character: ....

Best part of the book:

....

....

....

....

Favorite Quotes From the Book:

....

....

....

....

Source:

○ Bought ○ loaned

From ....

The book was easy to read

○ Yes   ○ No

Would you recommend
this book to a friend?

○ Yes   ○ No

Rating   ☆ ☆ ☆ ☆ ☆

○ Paperback ○ Hardback ○ Ebook ○ Audiobook

○ Non-fiction ○ Fiction

38

Started: .... Finished: ....

Book Title: ....

Author: ....

My Review

....

....

....

....

....

My Favorite Character: ....

Best part of the book:

....

....

....

....

Favorite Quotes From the Book:

....

....

....

....

Source:

○ Bought ○ loaned

From ....

The book was easy to read

○ Yes ○ No

Would you recommend this book to a friend?

○ Yes ○ No

Rating ☆ ☆ ☆ ☆ ☆

☐ Paperback ☐ Hardback ☐ Ebook ☐ Audiobook

☐ Non-fiction ☐ Fiction

39

Started: .... Finished: ....

Book Title: ....

Author: ....

My Review

....
....
....
....
....

My Favorite Character: ....

Best part of the book:

....

....

....

....

Favorite Quotes From the Book:

....

....

....

....

Source:

☐ Bought ☐ loaned

From ....

The book was easy to read

☐ Yes   ☐ No

Would you recommend
this book to a friend?

☐ Yes   ☐ No

Rating ☆ ☆ ☆ ☆ ☆

☐ Paperback ☐ Hardback ☐ Ebook ☐ Audiobook

☐ Non-fiction ☐ Fiction

40

Started: .... Finished: ....

Book Title: ....

Author: ....

My Review

....

....

....

....

....

My Favorite Character: ....

Best part of the book:

....

....

....

....

Favorite Quotes From the Book:

....

....

....

....

Source:

☐ Bought ☐ loaned

From ....

The book was easy to read

☐ Yes   ☐ No

Would you recommend this book to a friend?

☐ Yes   ☐ No

Rating ☆ ☆ ☆ ☆ ☆

○ Paperback ○ Hardback ○ Ebook ○ Audiobook

○ Non-fiction ○ Fiction

41

Started: .... Finished: ....

Book Title: ....

Author: ....

My Review

....

....

....

....

....

My Favorite Character: ....

Best part of the book:

....

....

....

....

Favorite Quotes From the Book:

....

....

....

....

Source:

○ Bought ○ loaned

From ....

The book was easy to read

○ Yes   ○ No

Would you recommend
this book to a friend?

○ Yes   ○ No

Rating ☆ ☆ ☆ ☆ ☆

◯ Paperback   ◯ Hardback   ◯ Ebook   ◯ Audiobook

◯ Non-fiction   ◯ Fiction

42

Started: ....   Finished: ....

Book Title: ....

Author: ....

My Review

....

....

....

....

....

My Favorite Character: ....

Best part of the book:

....

....

....

....

Favorite Quotes From the Book:

....

....

....

....

Source:

◯ Bought   ◯ loaned

From ....

The book was easy to read

◯ Yes   ◯ No

Would you recommend this book to a friend?

◯ Yes   ◯ No

Rating   ☆ ☆ ☆ ☆ ☆

☐ Paperback ☐ Hardback ☐ Ebook ☐ Audiobook

☐ Non-fiction ☐ Fiction

43

Started: .... Finished: ....

Book Title: ....

Author: ....

My Review

....

....

....

....

....

My Favorite Character: ....

Best part of the book:

....

....

....

....

Favorite Quotes From the Book:

....

....

....

....

Source:

☐ Bought ☐ loaned

From ....

The book was easy to read

☐ Yes   ☐ No

Would you recommend this book to a friend?

☐ Yes   ☐ No

Rating ☆ ☆ ☆ ☆ ☆

○ Paperback ○ Hardback ○ Ebook ○ Audiobook

○ Non-fiction ○ Fiction

44

Started: .... Finished: ....

Book Title: ....

Author: ....

My Review

....

....

....

....

....

My Favorite Character: ....

Best part of the book:

....

....

....

....

Favorite Quotes From the Book:

....

....

....

....

Source:

○ Bought ○ loaned

From ....

The book was easy to read

○ Yes   ○ No

Would you recommend
this book to a friend?

○ Yes   ○ No

Rating ☆ ☆ ☆ ☆ ☆

◯ Paperback ◯ Hardback ◯ Ebook ◯ Audiobook

◯ Non-fiction ◯ Fiction

45

Started: .... Finished: ....

Book Title: ....

Author: ....

My Review

....

....

....

....

....

My Favorite Character: ....

Best part of the book:

....

....

....

....

Favorite Quotes From the Book:

....

....

....

....

Source:

◯ Bought ◯ loaned

From ....

The book was easy to read

◯ Yes   ◯ No

Would you recommend
this book to a friend?

◯ Yes   ◯ No

Rating ☆ ☆ ☆ ☆ ☆

○ Paperback ○ Hardback ○ Ebook ○ Audiobook

○ Non-fiction ○ Fiction

46

Started: .... Finished: ....

Book Title: ....

Author: ....

My Review

....

....

....

....

....

My Favorite Character: ....

Best part of the book:

....

....

....

....

Favorite Quotes From the Book:

....

....

....

....

Source:

○ Bought ○ loaned

From ....

The book was easy to read

○ Yes   ○ No

Would you recommend
this book to a friend?

○ Yes   ○ No

Rating   ☆ ☆ ☆ ☆ ☆

☐ Paperback ☐ Hardback ☐ Ebook ☐ Audiobook

☐ Non-fiction ☐ Fiction

47

Started: .... Finished: ....

Book Title: ....

Author: ....

My Review

....
....
....
....
....

My Favorite Character: ....

Best part of the book:

....
....
....
....

Favorite Quotes From the Book:

....
....
....
....

Source:

☐ Bought ☐ loaned

From ....

The book was easy to read

☐ Yes ☐ No

Would you recommend this book to a friend?

☐ Yes ☐ No

Rating ☆☆☆☆☆

○ Paperback ○ Hardback ○ Ebook ○ Audiobook

○ Non-fiction ○ Fiction

48

Started: .... Finished: ....

Book Title: ....

Author: ....

My Review

....

....

....

....

....

My Favorite Character: ....

Best part of the book:

....

....

....

....

Favorite Quotes From the Book:

....

....

....

....

Source:

○ Bought ○ loaned

From ....

The book was easy to read

○ Yes ○ No

Would you recommend this book to a friend?

○ Yes ○ No

Rating ☆☆☆☆☆

☐ Paperback ☐ Hardback ☐ Ebook ☐ Audiobook

☐ Non-fiction ☐ Fiction

49

Started: .... Finished: ....

Book Title: ....

Author: ....

My Review

....

....

....

....

....

My Favorite Character: ....

Best part of the book:

....

....

....

....

Favorite Quotes From the Book:

....

....

....

....

Source:

☐ Bought ☐ loaned

From ....

The book was easy to read

☐ Yes   ☐ No

Would you recommend this book to a friend?

☐ Yes   ☐ No

Rating ☆ ☆ ☆ ☆ ☆

☐ Paperback ☐ Hardback ☐ Ebook ☐ Audiobook

☐ Non-fiction ☐ Fiction

50

Started: .... Finished: ....

Book Title: ....

Author: ....

My Review

....

....

....

....

....

My Favorite Character: ....

Best part of the book:

....

....

....

....

Favorite Quotes From the Book:

....

....

....

....

Source:

☐ Bought ☐ loaned

From ....

The book was easy to read

☐ Yes   ☐ No

Would you recommend
this book to a friend?

☐ Yes   ☐ No

Rating ☆ ☆ ☆ ☆ ☆

○ Paperback ○ Hardback ○ Ebook ○ Audiobook

○ Non-fiction ○ Fiction

51

Started: .... Finished: ....

Book Title: ....

Author: ....

My Review

....

....

....

....

....

My Favorite Character: ....

Best part of the book:

....

....

....

....

Favorite Quotes From the Book:

....

....

....

....

Source:

○ Bought ○ loaned

From ....

The book was easy to read

○ Yes   ○ No

Would you recommend
this book to a friend?
○ Yes   ○ No

Rating   ☆ ☆ ☆ ☆ ☆

☐ Paperback ☐ Hardback ☐ Ebook ☐ Audiobook

☐ Non-fiction ☐ Fiction

52

Started: .... Finished: ....

Book Title: ....

Author: ....

My Review

....

....

....

....

....

My Favorite Character: ....

Best part of the book:

....

....

....

....

Favorite Quotes From the Book:

....

....

....

....

Source:

☐ Bought ☐ loaned

From ....

The book was easy to read

☐ Yes   ☐ No

Would you recommend this book to a friend?

☐ Yes   ☐ No

Rating ☆ ☆ ☆ ☆ ☆

□ Paperback □ Hardback □ Ebook □ Audiobook

□ Non-fiction □ Fiction

53

Started: .... Finished: ....

Book Title: ....

Author: ....

My Review

....

....

....

....

....

My Favorite Character: ....

Best part of the book:

....

....

....

....

Favorite Quotes From the Book:

....

....

....

....

Source:

□ Bought □ loaned

From ....

The book was easy to read

□ Yes   □ No

Would you recommend
this book to a friend?

□ Yes   □ No

Rating ☆ ☆ ☆ ☆ ☆

☐ Paperback ☐ Hardback ☐ Ebook ☐ Audiobook

☐ Non-fiction ☐ Fiction

54

Started: .... Finished: ....

Book Title: ....

Author: ....

My Review

....
....
....
....
....

My Favorite Character: ....

Best part of the book:

....
....
....
....

Favorite Quotes From the Book:

....
....
....
....

Source:

☐ Bought ☐ loaned

From ....

The book was easy to read

☐ Yes ☐ No

Would you recommend this book to a friend?

☐ Yes ☐ No

Rating ☆ ☆ ☆ ☆ ☆

☐ Paperback ☐ Hardback ☐ Ebook ☐ Audiobook

☐ Non-fiction ☐ Fiction

55

Started: .... Finished: ....

Book Title: ....

Author: ....

My Review

....

....

....

....

....

My Favorite Character: ....

Best part of the book:

....

....

....

....

Favorite Quotes From the Book:

....

....

....

....

Source:

☐ Bought ☐ loaned

From ....

The book was easy to read

☐ Yes   ☐ No

Would you recommend
this book to a friend?

☐ Yes   ☐ No

Rating ☆ ☆ ☆ ☆ ☆

☐ Paperback ☐ Hardback ☐ Ebook ☐ Audiobook

☐ Non-fiction ☐ Fiction

56

Started: .... Finished: ....

Book Title: ....

Author: ....

My Review

....

....

....

....

....

My Favorite Character: ....

Best part of the book:

....

....

....

....

Favorite Quotes From the Book:

....

....

....

....

Source:

☐ Bought ☐ loaned

From ....

The book was easy to read

☐ Yes   ☐ No

Would you recommend this book to a friend?

☐ Yes   ☐ No

Rating ☆ ☆ ☆ ☆ ☆

- ☐ Paperback ☐ Hardback ☐ Ebook ☐ Audiobook
- ☐ Non-fiction ☐ Fiction

57

Started: .... Finished: ....

Book Title: ....

Author: ....

My Review

....
....
....
....
....

My Favorite Character: ....

Best part of the book:

....
....
....
....

Favorite Quotes From the Book:

....
....
....
....

Source:

☐ Bought ☐ loaned

From ....

The book was easy to read

☐ Yes   ☐ No

Would you recommend
this book to a friend?
☐ Yes   ☐ No

Rating ☆ ☆ ☆ ☆ ☆

○ Paperback ○ Hardback ○ Ebook ○ Audiobook

○ Non-fiction ○ Fiction

58

Started: .... Finished: ....

Book Title: ....

Author: ....

My Review

....

....

....

....

....

My Favorite Character: ....

Best part of the book:

....

....

....

....

Favorite Quotes From the Book:

....

....

....

....

Source:

○ Bought ○ loaned

From ....

The book was easy to read

○ Yes ○ No

Would you recommend this book to a friend?

○ Yes ○ No

Rating ☆ ☆ ☆ ☆ ☆

○ Paperback ○ Hardback ○ Ebook ○ Audiobook

○ Non-fiction ○ Fiction

59

Started: .... Finished: ....

Book Title: ....

Author: ....

My Review

....

....

....

....

....

My Favorite Character: ....

Best part of the book:

....

....

....

....

Favorite Quotes From the Book:

....

....

....

....

Source:

○ Bought ○ loaned

From ....

The book was easy to read

○ Yes   ○ No

Would you recommend
this book to a friend?

○ Yes   ○ No

Rating   ☆ ☆ ☆ ☆ ☆

☐ Paperback ☐ Hardback ☐ Ebook ☐ Audiobook

☐ Non-fiction ☐ Fiction

60

Started: .... Finished: ....

Book Title: ....

Author: ....

My Review

....

....

....

....

....

My Favorite Character: ....

Best part of the book:

....

....

....

....

Favorite Quotes From the Book:

....

....

....

....

Source:

☐ Bought ☐ loaned

From ....

The book was easy to read

☐ Yes   ☐ No

Would you recommend
this book to a friend?

☐ Yes   ☐ No

Rating ☆ ☆ ☆ ☆ ☆

☐ Paperback ☐ Hardback ☐ Ebook ☐ Audiobook

☐ Non-fiction ☐ Fiction

61

Started: .... Finished: ....

Book Title: ....

Author: ....

My Review

....

....

....

....

....

My Favorite Character: ....

Best part of the book:

....

....

....

....

Favorite Quotes From the Book:

....

....

....

....

Source:

☐ Bought ☐ loaned

From ....

The book was easy to read

☐ Yes   ☐ No

Would you recommend
this book to a friend?

☐ Yes   ☐ No

Rating ☆ ☆ ☆ ☆ ☆

☐ Paperback ☐ Hardback ☐ Ebook ☐ Audiobook

☐ Non-fiction ☐ Fiction

62

Started: .... Finished: ....

Book Title: ....

Author: ....

My Review

....

....

....

....

....

My Favorite Character: ....

Best part of the book:

....

....

....

....

Favorite Quotes From the Book:

....

....

....

....

Source:

☐ Bought ☐ loaned

From ....

The book was easy to read

☐ Yes   ☐ No

Would you recommend this book to a friend?

☐ Yes   ☐ No

Rating ☆ ☆ ☆ ☆ ☆

☐ Paperback ☐ Hardback ☐ Ebook ☐ Audiobook

☐ Non-fiction ☐ Fiction

63

Started: .... Finished: ....

Book Title: ....

Author: ....

My Review

....

....

....

....

....

My Favorite Character: ....

Best part of the book:

....

....

....

....

Favorite Quotes From the Book:

....

....

....

....

Source:

☐ Bought ☐ loaned

From ....

The book was easy to read

☐ Yes   ☐ No

Would you recommend
this book to a friend?

☐ Yes   ☐ No

Rating ☆ ☆ ☆ ☆ ☆

□ Paperback □ Hardback □ Ebook □ Audiobook

□ Non-fiction □ Fiction

64

Started: .... Finished: ....

Book Title: ....

Author: ....

My Review

....

....

....

....

....

My Favorite Character: ....

Best part of the book:

....

....

....

....

Favorite Quotes From the Book:

....

....

....

....

Source:

□ Bought □ loaned

From ....

The book was easy to read

□ Yes   □ No

Would you recommend
this book to a friend?

□ Yes   □ No

Rating   ☆ ☆ ☆ ☆ ☆

◯ Paperback ◯ Hardback ◯ Ebook ◯ Audiobook

◯ Non-fiction ◯ Fiction

65

Started: .... Finished: ....

Book Title: ....

Author: ....

My Review

....

....

....

....

....

My Favorite Character: ....

Best part of the book:

....

....

....

....

Favorite Quotes From the Book:

....

....

....

....

Source:

◯ Bought ◯ loaned

From ....

The book was easy to read

◯ Yes   ◯ No

Would you recommend
this book to a friend?

◯ Yes   ◯ No

Rating ☆☆☆☆☆

○ Paperback ○ Hardback ○ Ebook ○ Audiobook

○ Non-fiction ○ Fiction

66

Started: .... Finished: ....

Book Title: ....

Author: ....

My Review

....

....

....

....

....

My Favorite Character: ....

Best part of the book:

....

....

....

....

Favorite Quotes From the Book:

....

....

....

....

Source:

○ Bought ○ loaned

From ....

The book was easy to read

○ Yes   ○ No

Would you recommend
this book to a friend?

○ Yes   ○ No

Rating   ☆ ☆ ☆ ☆ ☆

○ Paperback ○ Hardback ○ Ebook ○ Audiobook

○ Non-fiction ○ Fiction

67

Started: .... Finished: ....

Book Title: ....

Author: ....

My Review

....

....

....

....

....

My Favorite Character: ....

Best part of the book:

....

....

....

....

Favorite Quotes From the Book:

....

....

....

....

Source:

○ Bought ○ loaned

From ....

The book was easy to read

○ Yes ○ No

Would you recommend this book to a friend?

○ Yes ○ No

Rating ☆ ☆ ☆ ☆ ☆

☐ Paperback ☐ Hardback ☐ Ebook ☐ Audiobook

☐ Non-fiction ☐ Fiction

68

Started: .... Finished: ....

Book Title: ....

Author: ....

My Review

....

....

....

....

....

My Favorite Character: ....

Best part of the book:

....

....

....

....

Favorite Quotes From the Book:

....

....

....

....

Source:

☐ Bought ☐ loaned

From ....

The book was easy to read

☐ Yes   ☐ No

Would you recommend
this book to a friend?
☐ Yes   ☐ No

Rating   ☆ ☆ ☆ ☆ ☆

○ Paperback ○ Hardback ○ Ebook ○ Audiobook

○ Non-fiction ○ Fiction

69

Started: .... Finished: ....

Book Title: ....

Author: ....

My Review

....

....

....

....

....

My Favorite Character: ....

Best part of the book:

....

....

....

....

Favorite Quotes From the Book:

....

....

....

....

Source:

○ Bought ○ loaned

From ....

The book was easy to read

○ Yes   ○ No

Would you recommend
this book to a friend?

○ Yes   ○ No

Rating ☆ ☆ ☆ ☆ ☆

○ Paperback ○ Hardback ○ Ebook ○ Audiobook

○ Non-fiction ○ Fiction

70

Started: .... Finished: ....

Book Title: ....

Author: ....

My Review

....

....

....

....

....

My Favorite Character: ....

Best part of the book:

....

....

....

....

Favorite Quotes From the Book:

....

....

....

....

Source:

○ Bought ○ loaned

From ....

The book was easy to read

○ Yes   ○ No

Would you recommend
this book to a friend?

○ Yes   ○ No

Rating ☆ ☆ ☆ ☆ ☆

☐ Paperback ☐ Hardback ☐ Ebook ☐ Audiobook

☐ Non-fiction ☐ Fiction

71

Started: .... Finished: ....

Book Title: ....

Author: ....

My Review

....
....
....
....
....

My Favorite Character: ....

Best part of the book:

....
....
....
....

Favorite Quotes From the Book:

....
....
....
....

Source:

☐ Bought ☐ loaned

From ....

The book was easy to read

☐ Yes   ☐ No

Would you recommend
this book to a friend?

☐ Yes   ☐ No

Rating ☆ ☆ ☆ ☆ ☆

○ Paperback ○ Hardback ○ Ebook ○ Audiobook

○ Non-fiction ○ Fiction

72

Started: .... Finished: ....

Book Title: ....

Author: ....

My Review

....
....
....
....
....

My Favorite Character: ....

Best part of the book:

....
....
....
....

Favorite Quotes From the Book:

....
....
....
....

Source:

○ Bought ○ loaned

From ....

The book was easy to read

○ Yes   ○ No

Would you recommend
this book to a friend?

○ Yes   ○ No

Rating ☆☆☆☆☆

☐ Paperback ☐ Hardback ☐ Ebook ☐ Audiobook

☐ Non-fiction ☐ Fiction

73

Started: .... Finished: ....

Book Title: ....

Author: ....

My Review

....

....

....

....

....

My Favorite Character: ....

Best part of the book:

....

....

....

....

Favorite Quotes From the Book:

....

....

....

....

Source:

☐ Bought ☐ loaned

From ....

The book was easy to read

☐ Yes   ☐ No

Would you recommend
this book to a friend?

☐ Yes   ☐ No

Rating ☆☆☆☆☆

○ Paperback ○ Hardback ○ Ebook ○ Audiobook

○ Non-fiction ○ Fiction

74

Started: .... Finished: ....

Book Title: ....

Author: ....

My Review

....

....

....

....

....

My Favorite Character: ....

Best part of the book:

....

....

....

....

Favorite Quotes From the Book:

....

....

....

....

Source:

○ Bought ○ loaned

From ....

The book was easy to read

○ Yes   ○ No

Would you recommend
this book to a friend?

○ Yes   ○ No

Rating   ☆ ☆ ☆ ☆ ☆

☐ Paperback ☐ Hardback ☐ Ebook ☐ Audiobook

☐ Non-fiction ☐ Fiction

75

Started: .... Finished: ....

Book Title: ....

Author: ....

My Review

....

....

....

....

....

My Favorite Character: ....

Best part of the book:

....

....

....

....

Favorite Quotes From the Book:

....

....

....

....

Source:

☐ Bought ☐ loaned

From ....

The book was easy to read

☐ Yes   ☐ No

Would you recommend
this book to a friend?

☐ Yes   ☐ No

Rating ☆ ☆ ☆ ☆ ☆

○ Paperback   ○ Hardback   ○ Ebook   ○ Audiobook

○ Non-fiction   ○ Fiction

76

Started: .... Finished: ....

Book Title: ....

Author: ....

My Review

....

....

....

....

....

My Favorite Character: ....

Best part of the book:

....

....

....

....

Favorite Quotes From the Book:

....

....

....

....

Source:

○ Bought ○ loaned

From ....

The book was easy to read

○ Yes   ○ No

Would you recommend
this book to a friend?

○ Yes   ○ No

Rating   ☆ ☆ ☆ ☆ ☆

☐ Paperback ☐ Hardback ☐ Ebook ☐ Audiobook

☐ Non-fiction ☐ Fiction

77

Started: .... Finished: ....

Book Title: ....

Author: ....

My Review

....

....

....

....

....

My Favorite Character: ....

Best part of the book:

....

....

....

....

Favorite Quotes From the Book:

....

....

....

....

Source:

☐ Bought ☐ loaned

From ....

The book was easy to read

☐ Yes   ☐ No

Would you recommend
this book to a friend?
☐ Yes   ☐ No

Rating ☆ ☆ ☆ ☆ ☆

○ Paperback ○ Hardback ○ Ebook ○ Audiobook

○ Non-fiction ○ Fiction

78

Started: .... Finished: ....

Book Title: ....

Author: ....

My Review

....
....
....
....
....

My Favorite Character: ....

Best part of the book:

....
....
....
....

Favorite Quotes From the Book:

....
....
....
....

Source:

○ Bought ○ loaned

From ....

The book was easy to read

○ Yes   ○ No

Would you recommend this book to a friend?

○ Yes   ○ No

Rating ☆ ☆ ☆ ☆ ☆

- ☐ Paperback ☐ Hardback ☐ Ebook ☐ Audiobook
- ☐ Non-fiction ☐ Fiction

79

Started: .... Finished: ....

Book Title: ....

Author: ....

My Review

....

....

....

....

....

My Favorite Character: ....

Best part of the book:

....

....

....

....

Favorite Quotes From the Book:

....

....

....

....

Source:

☐ Bought ☐ loaned

From ....

The book was easy to read

☐ Yes   ☐ No

Would you recommend
this book to a friend?

☐ Yes   ☐ No

Rating ☆ ☆ ☆ ☆ ☆

☐ Paperback ☐ Hardback ☐ Ebook ☐ Audiobook

☐ Non-fiction ☐ Fiction

80

Started: .... Finished: ....

Book Title: ....

Author: ....

My Review

....
....
....
....
....

My Favorite Character: ....

Best part of the book:

....
....
....
....

Favorite Quotes From the Book:

....
....
....
....

Source:

☐ Bought ☐ loaned

From ....

The book was easy to read

☐ Yes ☐ No

Would you recommend this book to a friend?

☐ Yes ☐ No

Rating ☆☆☆☆☆

☐ Paperback ☐ Hardback ☐ Ebook ☐ Audiobook

☐ Non-fiction ☐ Fiction

81

Started: .... Finished: ....

Book Title: ....

Author: ....

My Review

....

....

....

....

....

My Favorite Character: ....

Best part of the book:

....

....

....

....

Favorite Quotes From the Book:

....

....

....

....

Source:

☐ Bought ☐ loaned

From ....

The book was easy to read

☐ Yes   ☐ No

Would you recommend
this book to a friend?

☐ Yes   ☐ No

Rating   ☆ ☆ ☆ ☆ ☆

○ Paperback ○ Hardback ○ Ebook ○ Audiobook

○ Non-fiction ○ Fiction

82

Started: .... Finished: ....

Book Title: ....

Author: ....

My Review

....

....

....

....

....

My Favorite Character: ....

Best part of the book:

....

....

....

....

Favorite Quotes From the Book:

....

....

....

....

Source:

○ Bought ○ loaned

From ....

The book was easy to read

○ Yes   ○ No

Would you recommend
this book to a friend?

○ Yes   ○ No

Rating ☆ ☆ ☆ ☆ ☆

☐ Paperback ☐ Hardback ☐ Ebook ☐ Audiobook

☐ Non-fiction ☐ Fiction

83

Started: .... Finished: ....

Book Title: ....

Author: ....

My Review

....
....
....
....
....

My Favorite Character: ....

Best part of the book:

....
....
....
....

Favorite Quotes From the Book:

....
....
....
....

Source:

☐ Bought ☐ loaned

From ....

The book was easy to read

☐ Yes   ☐ No

Would you recommend
this book to a friend?

☐ Yes   ☐ No

Rating   ☆☆☆☆☆

○ Paperback ○ Hardback ○ Ebook ○ Audiobook

○ Non-fiction ○ Fiction

84

Started: .... Finished: ....

Book Title: ....

Author: ....

My Review

....

....

....

....

....

My Favorite Character: ....

Best part of the book:

....

....

....

....

Favorite Quotes From the Book:

....

....

....

....

Source:

○ Bought ○ loaned

From ....

The book was easy to read

○ Yes   ○ No

Would you recommend
this book to a friend?

○ Yes   ○ No

Rating   ☆☆☆☆☆

☐ Paperback ☐ Hardback ☐ Ebook ☐ Audiobook

☐ Non-fiction ☐ Fiction

85

Started: .... Finished: ....

Book Title: ....

Author: ....

My Review

....

....

....

....

....

My Favorite Character: ....

Best part of the book:

....

....

....

....

Favorite Quotes From the Book:

....

....

....

....

Source:

☐ Bought   ☐ loaned

From ....

The book was easy to read

☐ Yes   ☐ No

Would you recommend
this book to a friend?

☐ Yes   ☐ No

Rating   ☆☆☆☆☆

□ Paperback □ Hardback □ Ebook □ Audiobook

□ Non-fiction □ Fiction

86

Started: .... Finished: ....

Book Title: ....

Author: ....

My Review

....
....
....
....
....

My Favorite Character: ....

Best part of the book:

....

....

....

....

Favorite Quotes From the Book:

....

....

....

....

Source:

□ Bought □ loaned

From ....

The book was easy to read

□ Yes   □ No

Would you recommend
this book to a friend?

□ Yes   □ No

Rating ☆ ☆ ☆ ☆ ☆

○ Paperback ○ Hardback ○ Ebook ○ Audiobook

○ Non-fiction ○ Fiction

87

Started: .... Finished: ....

Book Title: ....

Author: ....

My Review

....

....

....

....

....

My Favorite Character: ....

Best part of the book:

....

....

....

....

Favorite Quotes From the Book:

....

....

....

....

Source:

○ Bought ○ loaned

From ....

The book was easy to read

○ Yes   ○ No

Would you recommend
this book to a friend?

○ Yes   ○ No

Rating   ☆ ☆ ☆ ☆ ☆

○ Paperback ○ Hardback ○ Ebook ○ Audiobook

○ Non-fiction ○ Fiction

88

Started: .... Finished: ....

Book Title: ....

Author: ....

My Review

....

....

....

....

....

My Favorite Character: ....

Best part of the book:

....

....

....

....

Favorite Quotes From the Book:

....

....

....

....

Source:

○ Bought ○ loaned

From ....

The book was easy to read

○ Yes   ○ No

Would you recommend
this book to a friend?

○ Yes   ○ No

Rating   ☆ ☆ ☆ ☆ ☆

☐ Paperback ☐ Hardback ☐ Ebook ☐ Audiobook
☐ Non-fiction ☐ Fiction

89

Started: .... Finished: ....

Book Title: ....

Author: ....

My Review

....
....
....
....
....

My Favorite Character: ....

Best part of the book:

....
....
....
....

Favorite Quotes From the Book:

....
....
....
....

Source:

☐ Bought ☐ loaned

From ....

The book was easy to read

☐ Yes   ☐ No

Would you recommend
this book to a friend?
☐ Yes   ☐ No

Rating ☆ ☆ ☆ ☆ ☆

☐ Paperback ☐ Hardback ☐ Ebook ☐ Audiobook

☐ Non-fiction ☐ Fiction

90

Started: .... Finished: ....

Book Title: ....

Author: ....

My Review

....
....
....
....
....

My Favorite Character: ....

Best part of the book:

....
....
....
....

Favorite Quotes From the Book:

....
....
....
....

Source:

☐ Bought ☐ loaned

From ....

The book was easy to read

☐ Yes   ☐ No

Would you recommend this book to a friend?

☐ Yes   ☐ No

Rating ☆ ☆ ☆ ☆ ☆

☐ Paperback ☐ Hardback ☐ Ebook ☐ Audiobook

☐ Non-fiction ☐ Fiction

91

Started: .... Finished: ....

Book Title: ....

Author: ....

My Review

....

....

....

....

....

My Favorite Character: ....

Best part of the book:

....

....

....

....

Favorite Quotes From the Book:

....

....

....

....

Source:

☐ Bought ☐ loaned

From ....

The book was easy to read

☐ Yes   ☐ No

Would you recommend this book to a friend?

☐ Yes   ☐ No

Rating ☆ ☆ ☆ ☆ ☆

○ Paperback ○ Hardback ○ Ebook ○ Audiobook

○ Non-fiction ○ Fiction

92

Started: .... Finished: ....

Book Title: ....

Author: ....

My Review

....

....

....

....

....

My Favorite Character: ....

Best part of the book:

....

....

....

....

Favorite Quotes From the Book:

....

....

....

....

Source:

○ Bought ○ loaned

From ....

The book was easy to read

○ Yes ○ No

Would you recommend this book to a friend?

○ Yes ○ No

Rating ☆ ☆ ☆ ☆ ☆

○ Paperback ○ Hardback ○ Ebook ○ Audiobook

○ Non-fiction ○ Fiction

93

Started: .... Finished: ....

Book Title: ....

Author: ....

My Review

....

....

....

....

....

My Favorite Character: ....

Best part of the book:

....

....

....

....

Favorite Quotes From the Book:

....

....

....

....

Source:

○ Bought ○ loaned

From ....

The book was easy to read

○ Yes   ○ No

Would you recommend
this book to a friend?

○ Yes   ○ No

Rating   ☆ ☆ ☆ ☆ ☆

○ Paperback ○ Hardback ○ Ebook ○ Audiobook

○ Non-fiction ○ Fiction

94

Started: .... Finished: ....

Book Title: ....

Author: ....

My Review

....

....

....

....

....

My Favorite Character: ....

Best part of the book:

....

....

....

....

Favorite Quotes From the Book:

....

....

....

....

Source:

○ Bought ○ loaned

From ....

The book was easy to read

○ Yes   ○ No

Would you recommend
this book to a friend?

○ Yes   ○ No

Rating   ☆ ☆ ☆ ☆ ☆

☐ Paperback ☐ Hardback ☐ Ebook ☐ Audiobook

☐ Non-fiction ☐ Fiction

95

Started: .... Finished: ....

Book Title: ....

Author: ....

My Review

....
....
....
....
....

My Favorite Character: ....

Best part of the book:

....
....
....
....

Favorite Quotes From the Book:

....
....
....
....

Source:

☐ Bought ☐ loaned

From ....

The book was easy to read

☐ Yes   ☐ No

Would you recommend
this book to a friend?

☐ Yes   ☐ No

Rating   ☆ ☆ ☆ ☆ ☆

○ Paperback ○ Hardback ○ Ebook ○ Audiobook

○ Non-fiction ○ Fiction

96

Started: .... Finished: ....

Book Title: ....

Author: ....

My Review

....

....

....

....

....

My Favorite Character: ....

Best part of the book:

....

....

....

....

Favorite Quotes From the Book:

....

....

....

....

Source:

○ Bought ○ loaned

From ....

The book was easy to read

○ Yes   ○ No

Would you recommend
this book to a friend?

○ Yes   ○ No

Rating ☆☆☆☆☆

- ☐ Paperback ☐ Hardback ☐ Ebook ☐ Audiobook
- ☐ Non-fiction ☐ Fiction

97

Started: .... Finished: ....

Book Title: ....

Author: ....

My Review

....
....
....
....
....

My Favorite Character: ....

Best part of the book:

....
....
....
....

Favorite Quotes From the Book:

....
....
....
....

Source:

☐ Bought ☐ loaned

From ....

The book was easy to read

☐ Yes   ☐ No

Would you recommend
this book to a friend?

☐ Yes   ☐ No

Rating ☆☆☆☆☆

☐ Paperback ☐ Hardback ☐ Ebook ☐ Audiobook

☐ Non-fiction ☐ Fiction

98

Started: .... Finished: ....

Book Title: ....

Author: ....

My Review

....

....

....

....

....

My Favorite Character: ....

Best part of the book:

....

....

....

....

Favorite Quotes From the Book:

....

....

....

....

Source:

☐ Bought ☐ loaned

From ....

The book was easy to read

☐ Yes   ☐ No

Would you recommend
this book to a friend?

☐ Yes   ☐ No

Rating   ☆ ☆ ☆ ☆ ☆

☐ Paperback   ☐ Hardback   ☐ Ebook   ☐ Audiobook

☐ Non-fiction   ☐ Fiction

99

Started: .... Finished: ....

Book Title: ....

Author: ....

My Review

....

....

....

....

....

My Favorite Character: ....

Best part of the book:

....

....

....

....

Favorite Quotes From the Book:

....

....

....

....

Source:

☐ Bought   ☐ loaned

From ....

The book was easy to read

☐ Yes   ☐ No

Would you recommend
this book to a friend?

☐ Yes   ☐ No

Rating   ☆ ☆ ☆ ☆ ☆

☐ Paperback ☐ Hardback ☐ Ebook ☐ Audiobook

☐ Non-fiction ☐ Fiction

100

Started: .... Finished: ....

Book Title: ....

Author: ....

My Review

....

....

....

....

....

My Favorite Character: ....

Best part of the book:

....

....

....

....

Favorite Quotes From the Book:

....

....

....

....

Source:

☐ Bought ☐ loaned

From ....

The book was easy to read

☐ Yes   ☐ No

Would you recommend
this book to a friend?

☐ Yes   ☐ No

Rating   ☆ ☆ ☆ ☆ ☆

Printed in Great Britain
by Amazon

46913420R10066